EARLY TO MID-INTERMEDIATE

Composer's Choice

GLENDA AUSTIN

ABOUT THE SERIES

The Composer's Choice series showcases piano works by an exclusive group of composers. Each collection contains classic piano pieces that were carefully chosen by the composer, as well as brand-new pieces written especially for the series. Helpful performance notes are also included.

WILLIS MUSIC

EXCLUSIVELY DISTRIBUTED BY

Hal•Leonard® CORPORATION

7777 W. BLUEMOUND RD. P.O. BOX 13819 MILWAUKEE, WI 53213

© 2013 by The Willis Music Co.
International Copyright Secured   All Rights Reserved

For all works contained herein:
Unauthorized copying, arranging, adapting, recording, Internet posting, public performance,
or other distribution of the printed music in this publication is an infringement of copyright.
Infringers are liable under the law.

Visit Hal Leonard Online at
www.halleonard.com

FROM THE COMPOSER

In this new collection you will find something old, something new, something borrowed, and something blue. When you become more familiar with the solos, I know you'll figure it out! (In case you need help, the "answers" are at the bottom of this page.)

Some of these pieces have been in print as Willis sheet music for years, but this year I was inspired to write two new solos: "Midnight Caravan" and "Valse Belle." I hope you enjoy them, too.

Glenda Austin

"Old" – *Chromatic Conversation, South Sea Lullaby,*
Etude in E Major, Tangorific, or *Reverie*

"New" – *Midnight Caravan, Valse Belle*

"Borrowed" – *Valse Belle*
(a homage to Bill Gillock)

"Blue" – *Blue Mood Waltz*

CONTENTS

MIDNIGHT CARAVAN

The rhythmic introduction of "Midnight Caravan" should set a mood of mystery. The single-note melody line in the right hand must be played with precision and punctuation, and diligent finger-work is required to play the entire piece in a clean, crisp way. Towards the end, there is a little relief from the driving rhythm with loud, crashing chords. However, the caravan soon gains speed again and disappears into the night!

SOUTH SEA LULLABY

A gentle rhythm and soothing harmonies permeate this tender lullaby. In trying to capture the Polynesian style, the left hand subtly plays a continuous rhythm typical of a tango. The right hand's legato melody in thirds may require slow, precise practice. The postlude at measure 33 seems to go on endlessly because of a series of deceptive whole note chord progressions that delay the final C Major cadence.

REVERIE

To the student: Don't be alarmed at seeing three staves! This piece is one of my favorites, and it really is easier than it looks. As the title implies, "Reverie" should be played dreamily with little sense of time. This languid quality may work in your favor because the left hand can cross over easily to complete the motif. Expert use of the pedal will also help to sustain the dotted half notes and contribute to that dream-like effect. (Teachers: This is a piece that an older beginner can play with great success!)

TANGORIFIC

Through the years I've heard this piece performed quickly and slowly. Both ways can be successful if the tempo remains stable throughout. The left hand is dominant in providing the tango rhythm, so it must be played in a secure and confident way. The right hand soars with a *cantabile* single-line melody. The dramatic height of "Tangorific" is the *allargando* (broadening in tempo) that builds into a grand *fortissimo*.

CHROMATIC CONVERSATION

"Chromatic Conversation" is a dialogue made up of chromatic fragments and scales that bounces back and forth between the hands. The form is A-B-A[1], and in both A sections, the eighth notes should be played evenly. In the B section, the hands stop the dialogue and speak together—the eighth notes are dotted and the rhythm swung, and the harmonies full of jazzy 7th chords. In A[1], the conversation returns to the single-note melody between hands and concludes with a slowly rolled, lingering E-flat 9th chord.

BLUE MOOD WALTZ

Commissioned by *Clavier*, the piece was reviewed by William Gillock. An excerpt:

> "…'Blue Mood Waltz' is basically Chopinesque. Its flowing melody, refined phrasing, and chromaticism recall the early 19th century, until a jazzy touch of humor intrudes at measure 6: a bar of feisty syncopation in the accompaniment. Another note of irreverence is the lowered seventh in the next to last measure… great fun for the adolescents for whom this is intended." (*Clavier*, October 1989)

ETUDE IN E MAJOR (EVENING TIDE)

The left hand controls the romantic melody throughout this entire etude. As the accompaniment, the right hand plays broken chords and may require separate, slow practice. To achieve tranquil fluidity, it would be wise to first practice without pedal and with a metronome. Experiment with *rubato* (literally, "robbed") by taking liberties with the articulation, dynamics and overall expressiveness. Think: **ocean waves!**

VALSE BELLE

"Valse Belle" could be subtitled *Hommage au Gillock*. It is my humble attempt at writing a piece reminiscent of the Gillock style. In typical 3/4 waltz meter, it is also an A-B-A[1] form with the A sections in C Major and the B section transcending several tonalities: E, A, C♯ Minor. Throughout, the right hand plays a melody of descending 7th chords while the left maintains a lilting waltz accompaniment.

Midnight Caravan

for Roxana Anklesaria

Glenda Austin

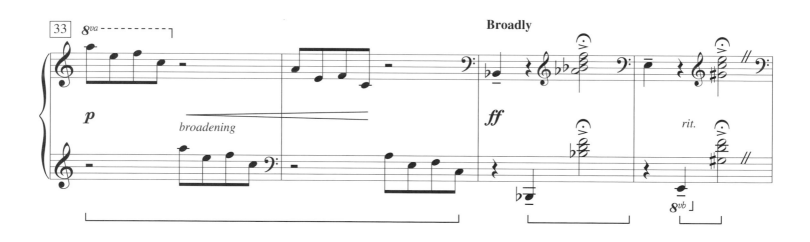

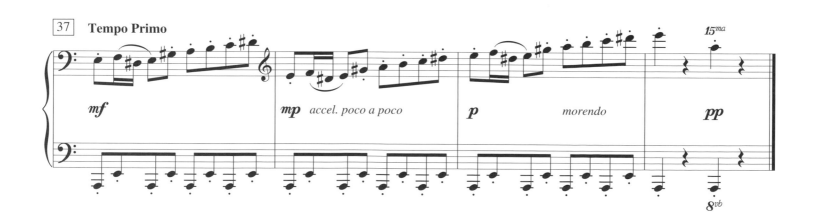

South Sea Lullaby

for Hiroko Yasuda

Glenda Austin

Gently, but rhythmically

Reverie

for Isaac

Glenda Austin

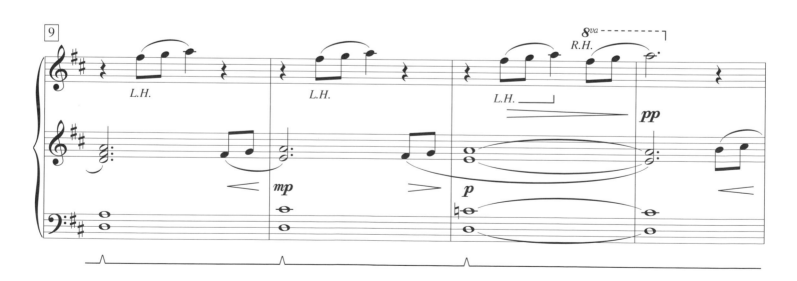

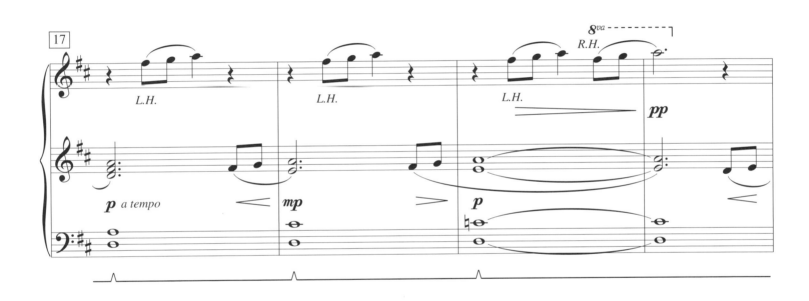

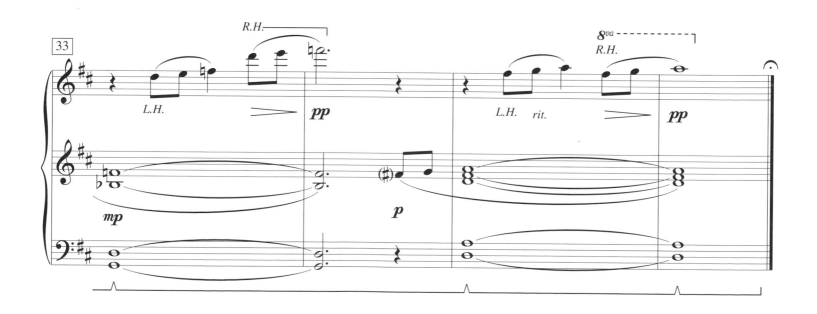

Tangorific

for Norma Holden

Glenda Austin

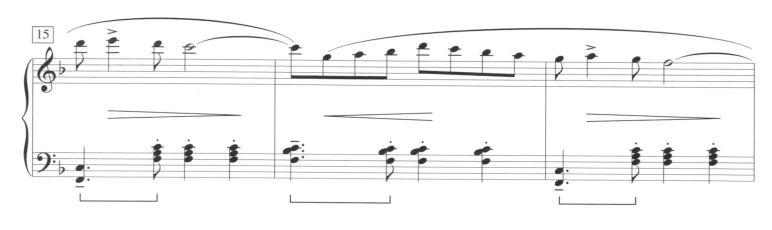

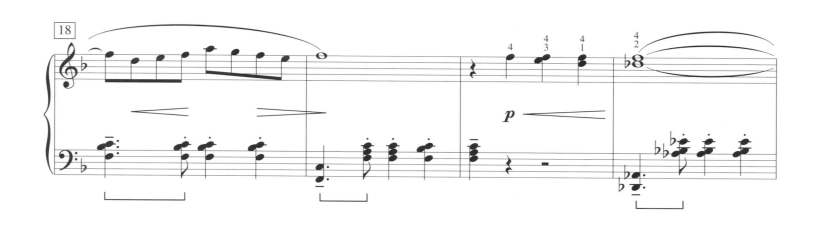

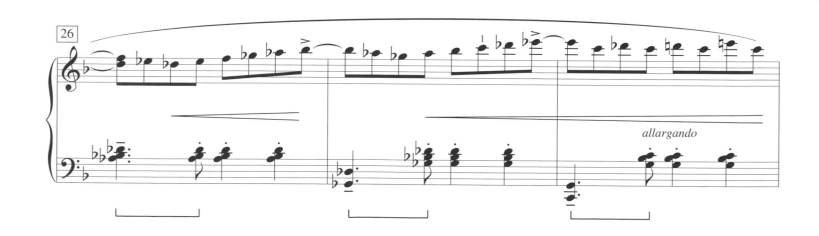

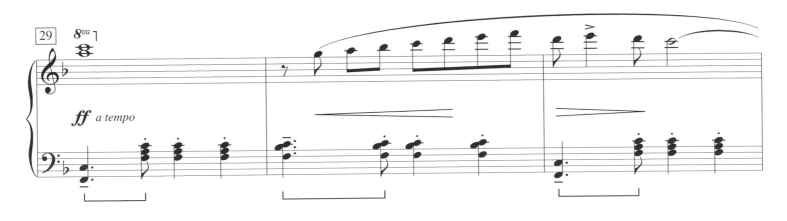

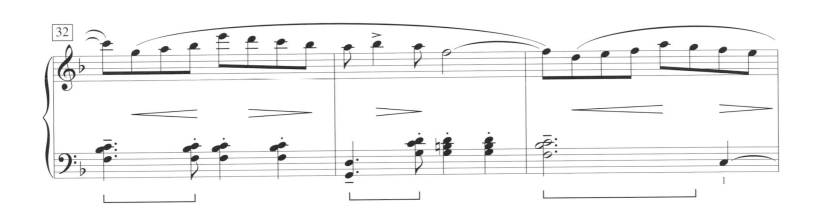

Chromatic Conversation

for Bill

Glenda Austin

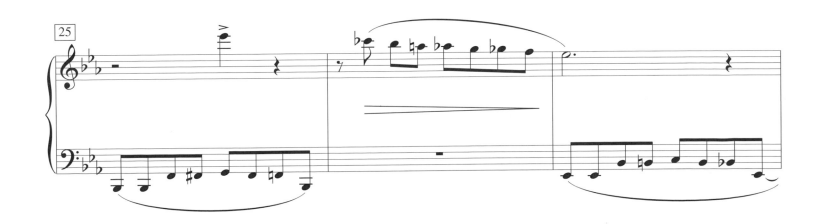

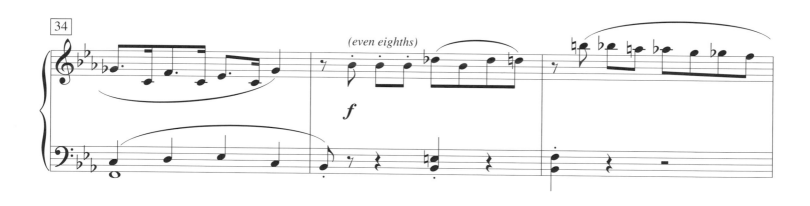

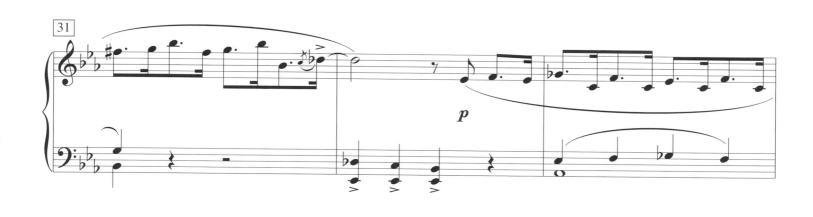

Blue Mood Waltz

Commissioned by *Clavier*

Glenda Austin

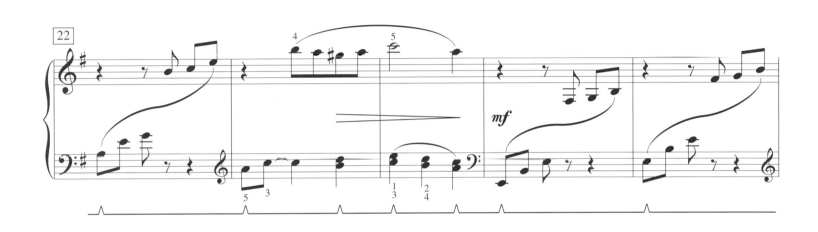

Etude in E Major
(Evening Tide)

for Gloria Sanborn

Glenda Austin

Molto tranquillo con rubato (♩ = c. 50-60)

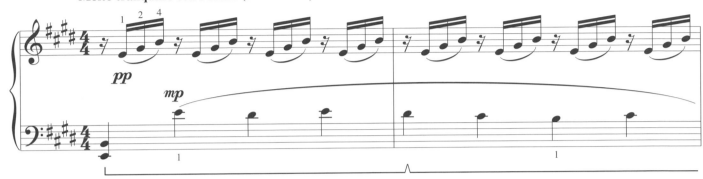

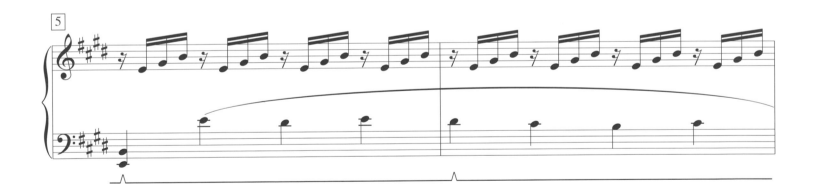

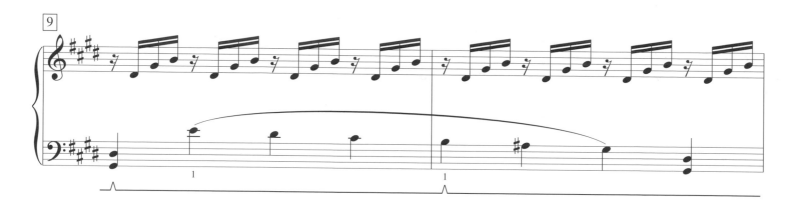

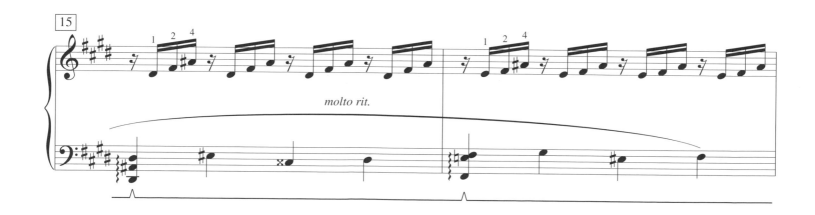

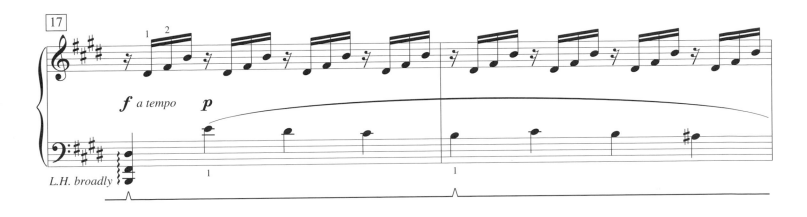

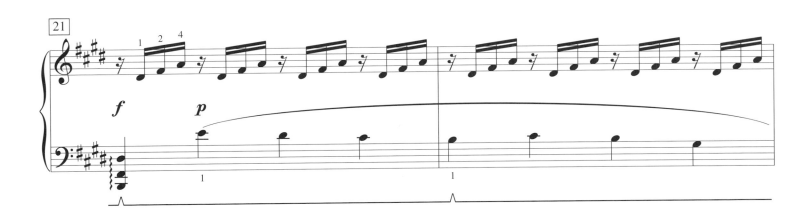

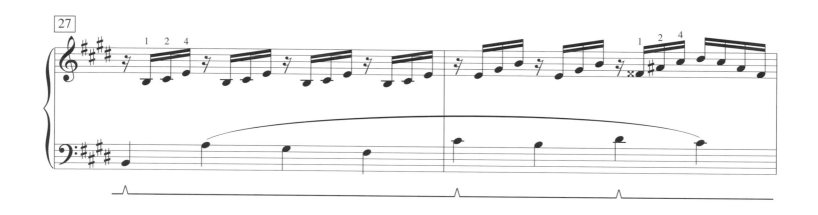

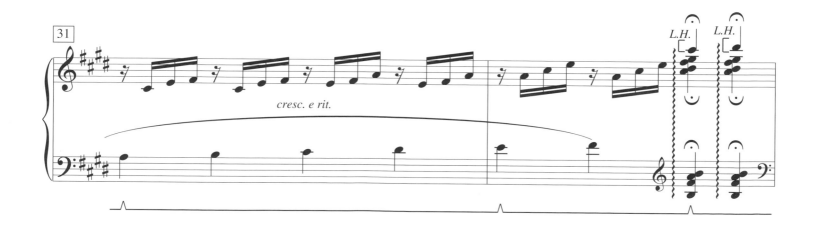

Valse Belle

for Kathleen Theisen

Glenda Austin